Travel Snapshots
AUSTRALIA

Text
Kelvin Aitken

Graphic Design
Patrizia Balocco

Map
Arabella Lazzarin

Contents

1 *The Koala with its soft fur and endearing gaze is a favorite with bushwalkers. Armed with sharp claws for climbing and extra padding to sit for hours on slender branches, the Koala is perfectly suited to an arboreal life.*

2-3 *Swept by the unceasing surf of the Pacific Ocean, One Tree Island on the Great Barrier Reef is a typical coral cay with its abundant marine and bird life. Shades of pale blue in the shallos of the lagoon contrast with the deeper blue of the open ocean.*

4-5 *Like crusty loaves fresh from the oven, the mounds of Kata Tjuta, or the Olgas, bake in the late afternoon light. Formed by erosion of vertical joints, Kata Tjuta is regarded as a sacred area by the Aborigines.*

6-7 *Bursting into life, a flock of waterbirds rise from their feeding grounds on the coastal wetlands of the Kakadu National Park in the Northern Territory. A haven for bird life, Kakadu is also famous for its reptiles, such as crocodiles, and pristine natural environment.*

8 *In north-west Australia, the Hamersley Ranges are not just rich in iron ore but also with the rugged beauty of Australia's outback. Apparently barren country holds a surprising number of animals, mainly reptiles.*

9 *Off the central coast of Queensland and protected by the outlying Great Barrier Reef lie the Whitsunday Islands. Seeking seclusion and peace, boats from private yachts to tourist ferries access beaches and bays on the scattered islands.*

12-13 *The city of Sydney overlooks the Opera House and Harbour Bridge. During the weekends pleasure craft emerge from sheltered bays to join container ships and ferries plying the sheltered waters of Port Jackson.*

14-15 *The convoluted bays of Port Jackson surround Sydney allowing ready access to boating and yachting enthusiasts. With city towers dominating the view, yachtsmen drill for a weekend regatta.*

16-17 *Softened by the late afternoon sun, a sand dune in the harsh desert area of south-west Queensland is a sculputre of beauty and light. Normally arid, the "Channel Country" can become a maze of rivers after heavy seasonal rains. Flowing south and joining to spread over millions of hectares the rivers isolate towns and make ground travel impossible. If there is enough rain the rivers may finally end at Lake Eyre, 480 miles away, in South Australia. Only three times in living memory has this lake been full. Normally an arid salt pan, Lake Eyre can be transformed into an orgy of bird life as the lake briefly blossoms into fertility.*

Published in North America by
AAA Publishing
1000 AAA Drive
Heathrow, Florida 32746
www.aaa.com

© 1993 White Star S.r.l.
Via Candido Sassone, 22/24
13100 Vercelli, Italy
www.whitestar.it

ISBN 1-56251-812-7
1 2 3 4 5 6 06 05 04 03 02

Printed in Singapore
Color separations by Magenta Lit. Con., Singapore

VAN DIEM GUL

DARWIN

ARNHE
LAND

KIMBERLEY •

BUNGLE BUNGLE
RANGE

NOR
TERR

MARBLE BAR • *GREAT SANDY DESERT*

NEWMAN •

TOM PRICE •

MACDONNELL

*HAMERSLEY
RANGES*

GIBSON DESERT

THE OLGAS

CARNARVON •

* *AYER

DIRK HARTOG
ISLAND •

MUSGRAVE RANG

WESTERN
AUSTRALIA

SOU
AUS

GREAT VICTORIA DESERT

NULLARBOR PLAIN

NAMBUNG
NATIONAL PARK
▲

• KALGOORLIE

• EUCLA

PERTH • *Swan River*

GREAT AUSTRALIAN BIGHT

Introduction

Kangaroos and Koalas, beer and barbecues, macho bushmen and tanned bikini-clad beauties. Such are the images that come to mind when Australia is mentioned. While all of these do exist, like all national stereotypes they fall short of encapsulating the substance of the country and its people. To understand Australia an examination of the past as well as the present, the environment and its effect on the inhabitants, is essential to grasp the essence that forms the land and its people into a nation.

The origins of modern Australia however are far from noble. Partly from nationalistic desires to expand and defend the British Empire, the first official visit by Europeans occured in 1770 when Zachary Hicks, cabin boy aboard the H.M.A.S. Endeavour, sighted the Australian mainland in what is now New South Wales. His captain, James Cook, turned the Endeavour north to explore the coast. Cook's visit was cursory and almost ended in disaster on the Great Barrier Reef when he ran aground and had to dump heavy cannons overboard to refloat his leaking ship. He spent 48 days in a sheltered river estuary which today has a town named Cooktown to commemorate the event. Only 17 years later, with no further survey or contact, the good judges of Old England decided to solve their burgeoning problem of convicted criminals, and to solidify the English right to the new continent, by sending 548 male and 188 female convicts with soldiers, sailers and administrators under Captain Arthur Phillip to establish a penal settlment in Port Jackson (later to be re-named Sydney Harbour).

Over the next 81 years roughly 162,000 convicts were sent to Australia to open up the land for exploitation and, not long after, to become unofficial slaves to the sheep farmers and settlers who braved the new continent to establish what Australia has become today.

Men and women punished by being sent to the colonies were guilty of crimes as diverse as muder or stealing a piece of lace. The first fleet to reach what was to become Sydney Harbour was beset with starvation and isolation. With additional fleets arriving with more convicts the modern city of Sydney slowly took form. Other penal colonies

were opened including the notorius Tasmania or Van Diemen's Land set up in 1804. It became the destination of the most uncooperative and notorious convicts and had a reputation of severity that increased as time passed. Tortuous work and severe conditions beyond our imagination were a daily reality for the 12,500 convicts that were sent there between 1830 and 1877. Mass graves and isolation experiments were part of the horror of early Tasmania.

Norfolk Island, off the coast of New South Wales, had a similar reputation with the convicts being beaten, whipped and killed at the whim of the Governor.

With such a short western history, it is easy to find just under the bustling "civilised" technological surface of the thriving modern Australian city the bones of events and systems that today would be decried as inhumane or even evil. Today the effects of such a past are still apparent. The tenacious adherence to "mateship", the sticking together no matter what trouble threatens, is a tenet harking back to the harsh days of warden, police and soldier against the hapless convict with no help beyond his peers. The modern Australian citizen would tend to proudly defy any form of authority, even if only superficially rather than bear the ostracism of "dobbing in" his mates. The modern psyche is also affected by the inferiority complex of a nation regarded as second rate by a patronising and sometimes arrogant colonising empire. With this in mind the modern Australians, with goals, dreams, ambitions, triumphs and determination in an often harsh environment becomes more understandable.

Every nation is influenced by their physical surroundings so it is interesting to see that while the Australian continent is approximately 2/3 the size of the United States, its total population of 17 million plus would fit into the city of New York. An examination of the population spread in Australia would show that the east and south-east coast, along with a pocket around Perth in Western Australia, hold 90% of the inhabitants with the remaining vast inland of the continent containing the balance. The casual observer may conclude that Australians do not like to be far from the beach. However, on closer examination it becomes clear that the physical structure of the continent has a great influence over the population density, food production, climate and, ultimately, the culture of its people.

The Great Dividing Range is a major feature of the eastern Australian landscape. From the tip of Cape

18 *Even with modern technology, the most reliable form of transport in the remote outback cattle stations is by horseback. Dodging snakes, charging bulls and rugged country, station horses are a valued asset.*

19 *Working in the tough cattle country of Central Australia can be heart breaking but is tempered with the unique sparse beauty of the remote landscape along with the comradeship of those who share a love of the land. Stockmen on horseback can be complemented by helicopters and four-wheel-drive vehicles in rounding up the herd in rugged country.*

York to the Grampians in Victoria 2,485 miles south, the Range separates the eastern seabord from the inland and outback. Forming plateaus and ranges that divide the warm moist coastal strip from the higher inland plains, the mountains provide a meterological and physical barrier that affects four states. From the heat and humidity of Cairns, the Great Dividing Range allows dairy cattle to browse on paddocks of rolling green a mere 18.6 miles away on the Atherton Tablelands. At the same time it effectively blocks seaborne moisture from moving inland to slack the thirst of the deserts. In New South Wales the change is just as dramatic with moist coastline and fertile farmland close to the range then gradually drying out into desert conditions further westward.

During the southern summer, winds blowing from the inland deserts bring temperatures well over 40 degrees celsius to the states of Victoria, South Australia and Western Australia. Running through three states is the Murray River which takes advantage of the desert heat to grow fruits and vegetables in the well irrigated lands bordering its meandering course.

The heart of the continent is taken up by seven main desert areas: the Tanami in the Northern Territory, the Simpson which is shared by Queensland and the Northern Territory, the Sturt Stony Desert in South Australia, the Great Victoria Desert running across South Australia and Western Australia and the Gibson and Great Sandy Deserts in Western Australia. These desolate areas are far from useless though as they are divided into reserves and cattle stations larger than some European countries and contain endemic wildlife that, together, are heart and soul of Australia.

From these desolate environments comes the dogged perseverance that marks the inland farmer who battles seasons or even years of drought, the comradeship of shared trials or conquests and above all a deep love for the harsh beauty of the Australian outback.
However, well before the first settlers arrived, the Aboriginal occupants had adapted to the diverse conditions in Australia. Leading a mostly nomadic lifestyle, the Aborigines lived in concert with the seasonal changes of weather and food reserves. Divided into 500 to 600 tribal groups across the country and speaking about 300 distinct languages, they developed their complex verbal culture and religion in isolation. Like most hunter-gatherers their technical achievements related solely to food gathering which included the woomera, a device enabling a spear to be thrown

over 360 feet, and the boomerang.

With the arrival of the first settlers came epidemics of disease such as tuberculosis, smallpox, measles, and influenza. Some settlers arranged hunting parties who further shot and killed any natives that could be found. Tasmania was one state whose history of abuse culminated in the eradication of every Aboriginal within a few decades of the settlers arrival.

Pushed into reserves, their complex social structures began to crumble. Well-meaning missionaries took children from their mothers to "educate" them adding to the demolition of their culture. Today a turning point has been reached with public education and opinion, not to mention legal rights and recognition, allowing the remaining Aborigines to re-claim traditional land with equal rights and opportunities as other Australian citizens.

The unique flora and fauna of Australia was a shock to the English and European settlers. With seasons reversed, their normal cold Decembers were suddenly hot to the extreme, the leaves stayed on the trees but the bark fell off, mammals hopped instead of walking and nursed young in pouches. The Platypus was laughed at as a taxonomic hoax by practical jokers and the scrub was alive with snakes as aggressive and venomous as any known.

Today the Kangaroo and Koala are internationally known symbols of the "Land down under". While New Guinea shares some of the marsupial or pouched animals, only in Australia can such a diverse family be found: from the huge Red Kangaroo, that grows taller than a man, to the tiny 12 inch Musky Rat Kangaroo. There is the stocky burrowing Wombat whose pouch opens in reverse to prevent the entry of loose soil; the Echidna and Platypus are the world's only Monotremes, mammals that lay eggs and suckle their young. Tasmania is the last refuge for the big marsupial predators. The sparky Tasmanian Devil along with the Eastern and Spotted Tail Quoll can be found there and some say that the Thylacine or Tasmanian Tiger did not become extinct in 1936 but can still be found in remote valleys of the interior.

The cute Koala was once hunted close to extinction for its soft fluffy coat but now enjoys protection along with most other endemic animals. Living high up among its sole food supply of certain eucalyptus leaves, the Koala today is threatened by disease and shrinking habitat. Unlike the Koala, kangaroos are still

hunted by licensed shooters with the meat sold as pet food or, in some states, gourmet cuisine.

Introduced animals have been the bane of the farming community with rabbit and mouse plagues regularly ravaging the countryside. Cane Toads were introduced to kill off the Cane-Borer Beetle but instead found different victuals and have increased into plague proportions. Feral cats have become a real danger to small endemic rodents and birds while introduced Sparrows, Starlings and Minahs have taken over the suburban environment abandoned by Cockatoos and Galahs. Introduced Buffalo are causing environmental damage in the rivers and billabongs or waterholes in the far north but at least they are exploited for their dark rich meat. Dingos were introduced by the first Aborigines but have adapted and become part of the native fauna.

The largest coral reef system on earth is found off the eastern coast of Queensland. The Great Barrier Reef stretches 1,243 miles from the tip of Cape York to Gladstone with associated smaller reefs appearing down to Lord Howe Island off New South Wales. Poisonous sea snakes inhabit some of the offshore reefs but fortunately they are more curious than dangerous and pose no threat to the thousands of visiting divers. Minke and Humpback Whales along with the world's largest fish (33-59 feet), the harmless Whale Shark, visit the outer reefs as well as the sister reefs in Western Australia.

Southern Right Whales, once hunted to the point of extinction, can be seen nursing their young during winter off the southern coastline. Here can be found the cold waters favoured by Abalone, the mollusc much loved by Asian customers and also the base for Australia's largest Tuna fisheries.

The people of Australia are a mixture of nationalities and backgrounds. Some are descendants of the first convicts and settlers, others are refugees from recent conflicts in near and distant countries. The one thing that they all have in common is that all are immigrants or descendants of immigrants. Chinese running to the southern goldfields or northern pearl beds, Greeks and Italians searching for a new life following the second world war, English looking for better opportunities and Slavs escaping an oppressive regime. Along with dozens of other nationalities they have blended their culture and cuisine to produce a healthy cosmopolitan community.

One of the main draws for the European

22 top Watsons Bay in Sydney is typical of the waterfront suburbs that line the convoluted bays of Port Jackson and Botany Bay. City living with ocean views and easy access makes Sydney Australia's most popular city.

22 bottom Australia's first permanent settlement has expanded to today multi-cultural metropolis. Parts of the early colony have been restored and retained in city boundary as a working section of the community.

23 A shopping arcade in Sydney displays wares from around the world. While wool carried Australian commerce for many years, local manufacturers have now to compete with clothing and technology imported from around the Pacific Rim and the United States. Producing only raw materials is no longer enough to compete on the world market.

24-25 *Crisp combers run up a remote sandy beach in South Australia. Many of Australia's coastal beaches are protected by delicate sand dunes whose stablishing influence is threatened by seaside developments. While the dunes are able to cope with storms rolling in form Antarctica, human intervention has been the cause of much coastal erosion. National parks have been provided to protect the more delicate coastal areas.*

immigrants was the work offered on the Snowy River Scheme. In 1949 the Snowy River Scheme commenced construction which diverted eastward flowing rivers back west via huge manmade tunnels bored through the mountains to provide cheap electricity and irrigation to the dry inland plains of New South Wales, Victoria and South Australia. Harsh working conditions, language barriers and families desperate for a new start in life led to a frontier style of life with laws losing their clear boundaries in the brash workers camps. The result was not just electrical and agricultural but it led to the cosmopolitan face of Australia.

Each group has brought their religion and customs with the result that it is not unusual to find a Moslem mosque in the same neighbourhood as a Roman Catholic Church, a Mormon temple with a Hindu shrine or an Anglican manse down the road from a Greek or Cypriot church. Toleration of others' beliefs is normal with the few rare difficulties traced back to prejudices in the countries of origin. While each national group treasures the freedom of politics, speech and religion found in Australia, each also acknowledges the value of remembering and passing on the cultural traditions of their respective home countries. Displays of nation dress, dance, art and drama are proudly demonstrated at public functions or parades with the young Australian-born taking the lead in national clubs and societies.

The cuisine from each country has impacted the staid, mainly English fare of roasts and pies that the early settlers brought with them so that today the current generation of Aussies will just as easily eat a meat pie with sauce as a Greek *gyros* with *tzatziki*, Italian pasta and pizza or an Indian curry with Arabic *tabbouleh* salad. While the American hamburger is a favourite, a Thai stir-fry or Chinese sweet and sour would also be a normal choice for a quick meal on the run.

Sport induces an almost religious fervour among the Australian people. During the cold winter months in the south, teams play a unique version of football called "Australian Rules". With dramatically different rules from normal football, the game appears to be a combination of rugby, soccer, basketball and Gaelic football. Blended together, it is a fast game of skill, with goals constantly being scored, making it a highly entertaining spectacle. It has been suggested that the game originated with the local Aborigines whose traditional game was adopted and adapted. Fans, from youngsters with faces painted in teams colours shivering in the rain to corporate executives tensely gripping their champagne in the heated and enclosed private boxes, watch and "barrack" with the fevour of zealots.

On the east coast the "Ironman" endurance race is based on the lifesaver's functions and covers swimming, rowing and running skills over an exhaustive water and beach course. Rugby League reaches a peak of popularity when each state plays their own team for the coveted trophy, giving vent to parochial displays of state pride. Of a more off-beat nature are diversions such as the Henly-on-Todd regatta. Held on the dry riverbed of the Todd River in the outback city of Alice Springs. The regatta is literally run with makeshift craft created by teams of sweating participants.

On an international scale cricket, soccer, golf, rowing, tennis, motor cycling, yachting, swimming and boxing are just some of the sports that have Australians leading the world giving credence to the fit athletic image credited to the nation. Every major Australian city can be found on the coast which partly explains the reputation of a nation of surfers and beach lovers. One reason for this is the segregation from all other nations by the oceans that surround the Australian continent. While the majority of the worlds countries can trade overland, Australia must cover vast distances across the oceans to exchange commodities. Discovered by sea, today the constraints of international trade dictate the continuing convenience of dwelling on the fertile outer edge of the island continent.

The gulfs, harbours and rivers that mark the location of each state's capital city are an asset exploited and enhanced by architecture and design. For example, in Sydney the Opera House and surrounding shoreline development allow full utilization of the light and seasons that decorate the changing harbour. In Melbourne, Port Phillip Bay is not just a body of water that must be traversed by container ships but is a huge playground for boats housed in large marinas, or water sports of all sorts launched from countless beaches that rim the bay's sweeping arms. Perth snuggles around the Swan River, a convenient rowing and boating haven while Brisbane's city boundaries are dictated by the twists of the river writhing towards the ocean. Adelaide abuts the white beaches along the Saint Vincent Gulf that swarm with swimmers during the summer while Hobart sits securely on the Derwent River whose expanding convoluted mouth forms Storm

Bay with its sheltered beaches and bays.

Towns and cities based solely on one activity, such as mining, are common in more remote areas. Kalgoorlic, a gold rush town in Western Australia, boasts the world's richest square mile. Sweeping up through the state are massive deposits of iron ore which are scooped from the earth in enormous quantities to fuel the coastal refineries. Cities and towns such as Newman, Tom Price and Marble Bar (a town holding the world record for continuous temperatures over 38 degrees celsius) in the Pilbara region attract adventures eager to share in the massive wealth that seems to be now found in only the most isolated areas. Argyle, an area in the oppressively hot and humid Kimberley Ranges near the border of the Northern Territory, has recently produced the rare, luscious, pink diamond. Coober Pedy, in South Australia, is the capital of the opal mining industry. Opals are a beautiful gem with the most stunning and valuable being the Black Opal which is a lustrous black with flecks of fire and rainbow glinting from the depths. With temperatures soaring into the 50's locals have found it more comfortable to build their homes underground. Far from being just grubby holes, the homes are cool and well lit with all of the modern amenties found in normal homes.

Lacking the antiquity of ancient civilisations that are the norm in other continents, Australia is blessed with a neophyte freshness as it forges ahead while finding its own feet in the international family. Freed from the constraints of tradition and convention, resistance against the inherited apron strings of England's monarchy, and America's more recent military protection, is common and no doubt they will be broken as the nation enters adolescence. Parallel with that movement are the yearnings of the Aboriginal people to rediscover their past, a difficult task with a mainly verbal history broken by the recent oppression and dislocation of native society.

Australia is a land of hope. With countries in the northern hemisphere reeling from pollution and exhausted natural resources, this young nation has only just scraped the surface of its rich mineral assets. Wiser from observing the decimation of fishing and animal wealth in neighbouring nations, Australia is tending towards sensible long-term management instead of short-term gains.
With diverse and unique wildlife coupled with a landscape of vivid contrasts, the nation celebrates the unique privilege of savouring the guadianship of the smallest continent.

Outback: the beauty of isolation

26 top *A marine research station along with a simple resort on Heron Island offers a unique holiday destination on the Great Barrier Reef. Visitors share the coral cay with sea-birds who nest in the Pisonia trees, on coral rubble or in underground burrows. In summers, Loggerhead and Green Turtles lumber up the beach to lay their eggs. Resident rangers run programs to explain the complex ecosystem that makes up the Barrier Reef and its cays.*

26 bottom *Cradle Mountain and Lake Saint Clair National Park in Tasmania are best explored on foot over the 60 miles of hiking trails crossing the mountains. During winter, snow turns the center of Tasmania into a cross country skiers wonderland. The interior is mostly rugged mountains and bush. Almost constant rainfall on the higher peaks feed rivers such as the Franklin and Gordon. Shrouded in controversy over proposed damming for a hydro - electric scheme, the rivers are an adventurous, sometimes dangerous, yet always spectacular way to see the interior.*

27 *The Pilbra region in Western Australia is split by the Hamersley Ranges. Cool Waters in Dales Gorge contrast the baking, iron-rich rocks of the cliffs. Lying beyond the normal reach of the northern wet season, the only water to fall here is during the rare visit by a monsoon that may be blown in from the coast. While many spectacular and interesting areas can be accessed by normal car travel, most of the Australian wonders and treasures can only be reached with specialized vehicles, airplanes or on foot. Taking the time to walk around an area such as Dales Gorge allows the visitor time to see the various life forms, both flora and fauna, that complement the outlandish landscape.*

28-29 *Low lying scrub and spinifex grass dot the plains of the Little Sandy Desert in Western Australia after recent rains. Early explorers suffered many hardships with not a few dying in their attempts to discover inland oceans, mountains of gold or fertile plains. Yet the nomadic Aboriginals were able to live in the superficially barren interior by adapting to the seasonal changes and using food sources such as grubs and reptiles that the explorers snubbed as inedible.*

29 top *Australia boasts more marsupials (using a pouch rather than a placenta and womb) than any other country in the world. Many are rare and endangered such as this Rabbit-Eared Bandicoot peeking from its desert burrow. Feral cats and other introduced species have added to the decimation or, at times, the extinction of endemic animals.*

29 middle *Spinifex grass can withstand high temperatures, drought and fire. The ring shaped appearance of this clump in Western Australia indicates its age. Once the ring reaches a certain size it begins to break up, forming small clumps on the outer circle. These then begin to form circles again thereby covering bare ground, protecting the soil from erosion and providing cover for wildlife.*

29 bottom *The long tail of the Kangaroo is used as a conterbalance when hopping at up to 30 miles per hour across rough country. A Wallaby is a smaller species and a Wallaroo prefers rocky habitats. Their ability to jump over the tallest fence made then unusable as domestic stock, even though their meat is quite palatable.*

Echoes of the Dreamtime

30-31 *Cast like playthings on a flat plain, the Devil's Marbles rock formations lie close to the geographic centre of Australia. Formed by wind, sun and rain erosion, the rocks decorate a wide area close to the Sturt Highway which runs from Darwin to Adelaide.*

31 *Silence spreads with the advancing shadows at dusk over sand dunes near Eucla on the Nullarbor Plain, a beautiful but desolate area on the southern coast. Nullarbor comes from the Aboriginal word meaning "without trees". The plains, which run the full width of the Great Australian Bight, are formed out of limestone creating massive underground water-filled caves and tunnels.*

32-33 *The upper reaches of Dales Gorge shows the contrast between the dry plains and cool billabongs. The nomadic Aborigines survived in a harsh landscape such as this, that defeated many settlers, by moving with the seasons and using the occasional permanent water supply as way stations. In places of special spiritual significance, rock paintings were left on the cliffs or the bones of dead relatives would be wrapped in bark and left in a secluded area.*

The red heart of Australia

34 top *Many areas of Uluru have special significance in Aboriginal initiation or dreamtime religious cermonies and therefore are not accessed by tourists. Recently Uluru was handed back to its traditional owners, or more accurately: custodians, who have stopped rampant commercial exploitation of the area and reestablished the ancient sacred sites. Climbing the rock is an arduous and, for the physically unfit, dangerous procedure. The view and cool breezes at the top make the effort worth while.*

34 bottom *The moods and colours of Uluru that change with the sun and seasons are mimicked by Kata Tjuta, or the Olgas, on the horizon. When the rains come, waterfalls cascade down the cliff faces eroding the vertical markings and clefts that mark the face of Uluru. The earth greedily soaks up all moisture allowing the low growing vegetation to survive the long dry season.*

34-35 *Christened "Ayers Rock" by early explorers, today Australia's second largest monolith is known by the Aboriginals earlier name of Uluru. Jutting from the surrounding plains, Uluru sits in the very centre of Australia like a massive heart and has an immensly important spiritual position in the Aboriginal culture. Late in the afternoon the setting sun plays tricks with the rock, turning it into the colour of blood, possibly bright orange or later a deep purple.*

36 *Like knobbly knuckles protruding from the earth, Kata Tjuta (The Olgas) glows with an inner heat in the cooling evening air. At night the temperature of the surrounding desert may plummet to freezing point.*

37 *Rising from the desert plains, various anomalies such as Mount Ebenezer, Uluru or here, Kata Tjuta, provided spiritual and cultural meeting places for the nomadic Aboriginal tribes. Even after recent rains the plains are a dull brown while the air is tinged with the red desert dust. Camel safaris and hot air ballooning provide a different slant to the outback experience.*

38-39 *Grasses and shrubs in the Amphitheatre at the Finke River Gorge National Park emphasise the beauty of the central desert areas. Once an inland sea, the Finke River contains a unique area called Palm Valley where tropical palm trees survive from an ancient sea-side grove.*

40-41 *The slow moving Thorny Devil is a unique spectacle with its armour of spikes that protect it from predators as it feeds on a diet of ants. Never actively drinking, this reptile collects dew and rainwater on its skin which moves by capillary action to the mouth. The 360 Australian lizard species vary in size from the tiny Skink to the 8 foot Giant Perentie, second in size only to the Indonesian Komodo Dragon.*

42-43 *Situated near Alice Springs in the Northern Territory, the McDonnel Ranges are the result of a fault that provide spectacular aerial views that are rivalled only by trekking by foot into some of the deep gorges and clefts formed in the rugged terrain. Many are accessible by road including Ormiston Gorge, Simpsons Gap with its tiny frogs hiding in cool crevices, and Glen Helen Gorge.*

The spectacular rocky scenery

44 Like stacked hats or bee hives, the Bungle Bungle Range lies on the south-east edge of the Kimberly area of northwestern Australia. Oppressive heat and rugged terrain make aeroplanes the most practical way of viewing the spectacular eroded formations. A very rough track part way into the range gives hikers the opportunity to see some of the formations first hand though the soft crumbling limestone makes climbing the domes dangerous.

45 Gosse's Bluff is actually an impact structure from the collision of a huge meteorite. The force required to cause such an impact is mind boggling. This formation and event is not rare as other impact craters exist across Australia, including the Henbury Metorite Craters near Uluru.

46-47 An eerie eroded landscape forms the Pinnacles in Nambung National Park. Situated on the coast north of Perth, wind and rain erode the sand dunes leaving calcified formations.

A land sculptured by water

48 Thirty-three foot tides drain huge bays such as King Sound near Derby leaving mud flats to shimmer in the oppressive heat. The entire north-west coast has the same massive tidal fluctuation which has led to tidal power generation experiments, incoming tides can overtake a running man. Climate and nutrient rich waters make the northern coastal area a perfect oyster farming location and pearl farms produce lustrous gems in honey, silver, white and precious black.

49 Salt lakes shimmer in the sun at Lake Lefroy Goldfields. Even in the most inhospitable areas marine, animal and bird life can be found that have adapted to the prevailing and changeable conditions.

50-51 Mongers Lake, one of dozens of lakes north and east of Perth, has its shores softened by blooming wild flowers. Varying in size, the lakes expand and contract, sometimes out of existence, depending on the rainfall.

52-53 The East Alligator River winds between sandstone outcrops in Kakadu National Park. Sitting between Darwin and Arnhem Land (an Aboriginal reserve) Kakadu has three main rivers running through it. Water Buffalo were introduced into Australia during the 1800's and have become a pest destroying fragile billabong and river systems. Culling in Kakadu and northern wetlands has been encouraged with the creation of a market for the dark meat.

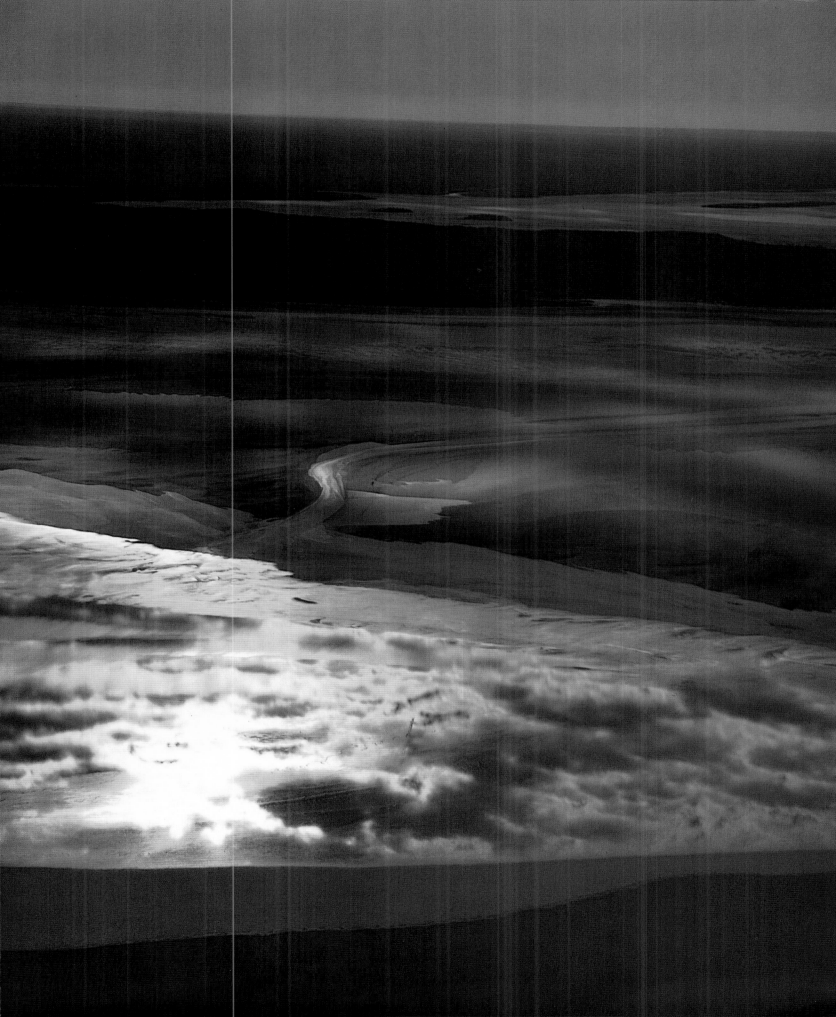

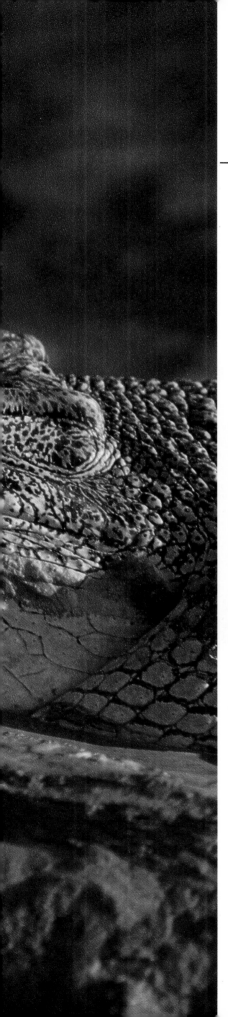

Wildlife treasures

54-55 *A young Salt Water Crocodile basks in the humid northern sun. "Salties" are the most dangerous of the two crocodile species in Australia. Ranging from off-shore reefs to inland creeks and billabongs, they have been responsible for the deaths of many swimmers. Growing to over twenty-four feet, the Salt Water Crocodile was once hunted close to extinction but is now under protection, becoming a dangerous nuisance in some northern populated areas. Crocodile farms are becoming popular and profitable with the skins being used for fashion accessories and the meat sold in trendy restaurants. The Johnson or Freshwater Crocodile is smaller, less aggressive and would tend to avoid rather than attack a human.*

55 *Covering a vast area in the Northern Territory, Kakadu National Park is home to a bewildering variety of life. Rangers can reveal unnoticed wonders of bird and animal life with an enthusiasm undimmed by years of experience. Due to careful management, the park - ranging from inland stone escarpments with rainforest and waterfalls to the swamps and billabongs on the coasts - remains unchanged over the millenia.*

56 A pair of curious Dingos attack a Perentie or Goanna. The Perentie is also considered a tasty meal for bushmen and Aboriginals, with a fine meat similar to chicken. It is assumed that the Dingo was introduced into Australia with the arrival of the first Aboriginals and is now regarded as indigenous. Due to their attacks on sheep a six thousand mile-long Dingo fence was built across three states to prevent northern Dingos replacing southern animals that were culled.
The fence is a massive affair, four times the length of the Great Wall of China, and is constantly patrolled by boundary riders.

57 A pair of Emus strut across grassy plains on Wilson's Promontory, a National Park south of Melbourne in Victoria. Widely distributed throughout Australia, the Emu is a flightless bird with a chesty booming call that lives in family groups. Similar to the African Ostrich, Emus are speedy runners and can deliver a powerful kick when threatened. Their eggs are gathered on a limited basis by a few licenced collectors and are carved by skilled artists into exquisite curios. Wilson's Promontory, the southern-most point in Australia, boasts a wide variety of common and endangered species in a spectacular granite landscape.

58-59 A pair of Red Kangaroos browse in a grassy meadow. Growing taller than a man the "Big Red" is the largest marsupial in the world, and lives in "mobs" of up to 100. Using its tail as a third leg to rest upon when feeding, it can accelerate at a tremendous rate when its keen hearing picks up any sign of danger. Despite the fact that they have been killed in their millions by farmers protecting the pastures of introduced sheep and cattle, Kangaroo mobs still exist in numbers that allow licenced cullers to shoot thousands each year for meat and skins. A joey, or baby Kangaroo, that survives the death of its mother is easily calmed by placing it in a bag, a surrogate marsupial pouch. The female is able to delay birth of its young in time of drought until fresh rains bring enough food to assure its survival. When a Kangaroo is born, it is blind and naked and instictively climbs into the pouch attaching itself to the mother's teat.

60 *The Great Dividing Range influences the climate along the entire eastern coast. Here Eucalyptus trees grow with Banksia and Bracken Ferns where sea-borne air is captured and deposited by rising buttresses and slopes on the eastern side of the range in New South Wales.*

61 *In Queensland the eastern side of the Range harbours lush tropical rainforests, in stark contrast to the dry inland plains. Parasitic vines, rare orchids and the homely Scrub Turkey live in the luxuriant and delicate rainforest canopy.*

62-63 *Viewed from the aptly named Echo Point, the Three Sisters rock formation in the Blue Mountains, west of Sydney, and part of the Great Dividing Range, glow in the afternoon sun. The mountains take their name from the blue haze that clothes the distant peaks.*

The Great Barrier Reef: pearls in the Pacific

64-65 Situated off Gladstone in Queensland, the Bunker Group of islands is part of the Capricornia section of the Great Barrier Reef Marine Park. Boult Reef (top) and Hoskyn Islets (bottom) come under strict visitor control due to their fragile ecosystems of sea-bird and turtle-nesting sites. Nearby Lady Musgrave (right) allows visitors, on day trips or for longer periods in the camping facilities, to explore the wonders both above and below the Great Barrier Reef. These are not islands but are sand cays, the result of wind and wave action depositing coral debris and sand on the reef. Birds use the rubble mounds to build their nests. Coupled with seeds borne to the reef by currents and offshore winds a small mound develops, eventually growing into a cay that can support fully grown trees.

66-67 Shades of blue pattern the outer edge of the Great Barrier Reef. Stretching 1500 miles from New Guinea to Gladstone, it is one of the seven wonders of the world. Made up of various reefs, cays and islands, the reef contains a vast array of life forms. For all of its size it is a fragile ecosystem able to endure the fiercest cyclone but susceptible to pollution and sediment from mainland rivers. Following the full moon in November or December, a mass spawning occurs among the corals. Lasting for about a week, the result is large pink slicks of eggs on the surface which provide food for plankton and baitfish who in turn are eaten by larger creatures including Manta Rays and Whale Sharks.

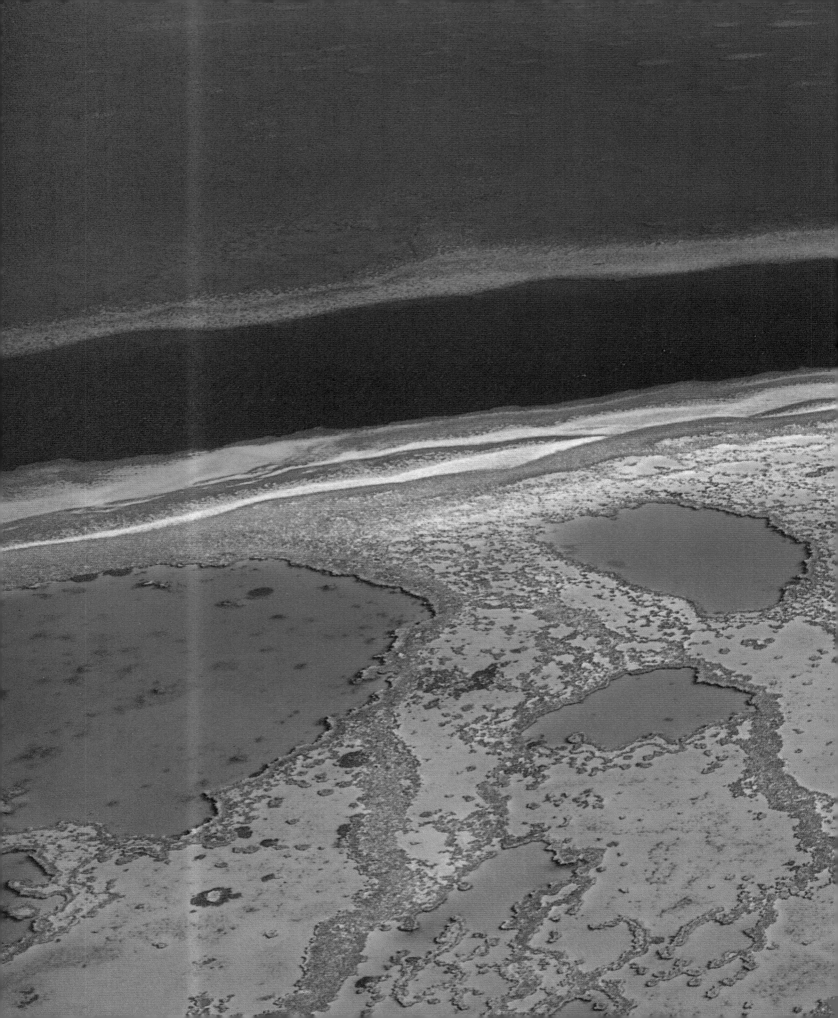

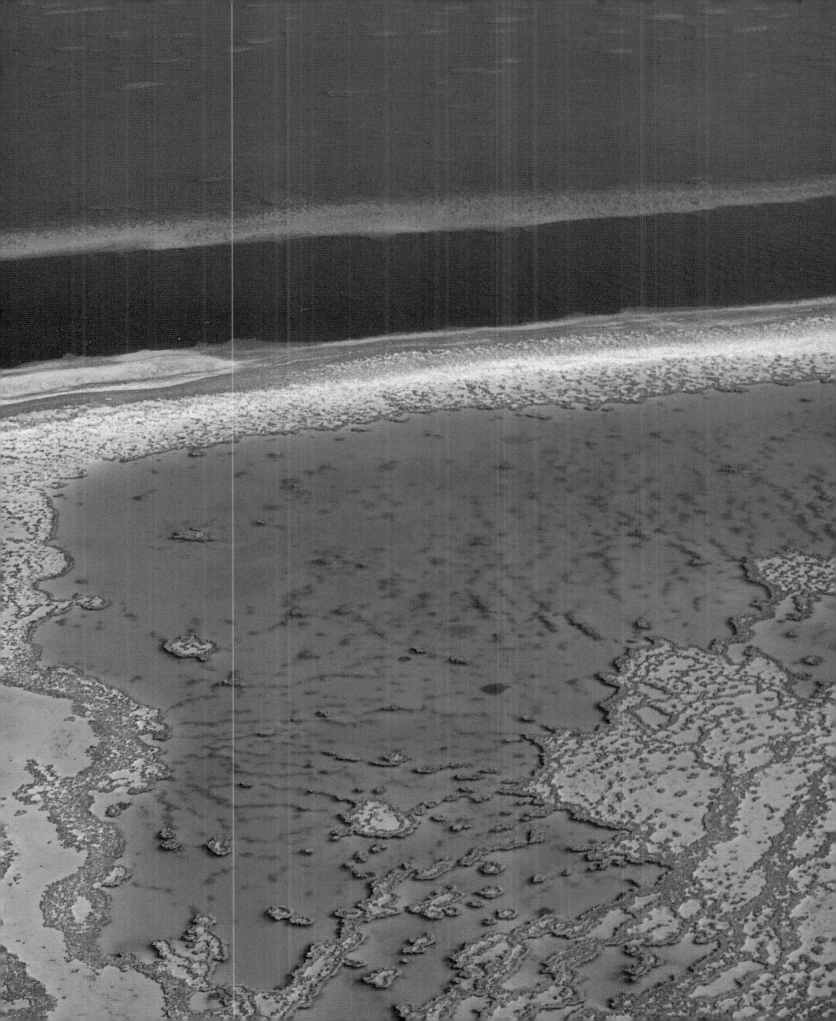

Marine marvels

68 top *The deadly air breathing sea snake is common on many reefs. However, their curious and friendly approach, along with a mouth too small to bite a diver, makes for an entertaining encounter. Comprising approximately 30 species, the sea snakes sleep under ledges and feed on small fish that are caught amongst the coral. Considered harmless despite their venom, most encounters involve the snake cheerfully watching its reflection in a diver's mask or sniffing around the diver's fins before sauntering off.*

68 bottom *Many reef fish, and the corals themselves, display brilliant colours such as this gorgeous Harlequin Tuskfish. Many reefs are now protected from fishing pressure resulting in prolific schools of fish accepting the diver as part of their environment, leading to mutually curious encounters.*

69   Growing on the outer reef face or in
passages with strong currents are
Gorgonian Sea Fans. Filtering the water
for food particles, the fans attain
enormous proportions in the deeper
waters that are unaffected by surface
waves and storms. Each fan is a world in
itself with a community of shells, crabs
and fish sheltering in its branches.
However, sea fans are not reef -building
corals. That is left to the stony corals
found only in shallow waters.

70-71   Gregarious by nature, Potato
Cod can reach 6 feet and 220 pounds.
North of Cairns on the outer Barrier
Reef is the Cod Hole, a dive site of
international renown frequented by Cod
and huge Moray Eels that delight in
human contact. A furious feeding session
with the cod acting like spoilt children
ends in contented pats and cuddles. The
eels, as fat as a man's thigh and longer
than the six feet protruding from the
rocks, enjoy the human touch as well.

72-73   The largest feared predator on
earth, the Great White Shark, is found
mainly around the offshore islands of
South Australia. Adventurers flock to
photograph this magnificent animal
during the summer months when it
ventures into southern islands to feed on
breeding sea lions and seals. Protected by
cages of steel or aluminium mesh, divers
can enjoy in total safety a view of an
unfettered oceanic predator. Blamed for
many and responsible for some attacks,
the Great White has a reputation for
savagery that becomes fallacious when
observed in its own natural habitat
without the torment of harpoons and
hooks.

The wonder zone:
where Earth meets the Pacific Ocean

74 *Sand shoals sculpt a river mouth on Whitehaven Beach. Due to a low population density in Australia, it is still possible to find islands and beaches that are unoccupied by towns, resorts, marinas and their associated crowds.*

75 *The Whitsunday Islands were first seen by Captain Cook in 1770 on Whit Sunday. Containing 74 islands, the group lies close to the mainland offering easy access to boating and fishing enthusiasts. Sprinkled with white coral sand, the beaches are protected by the outlying Great Barrier Reef and remain popular stop-over sites for travelling yachts and local "bare-boat" charters.*

Life in contact with the ocean

76-77 *Stanwell Park is the first of many coastal towns south of Sydney enjoying a mild climate all year round. Most have a history of fishing and farming but today the towns are sought out by city dwellers as the sites to build their "weekend" or "holiday" homes.*

77 *The narrow entrance of Port Jackson protects Sydney's harbour from the full violence of Pacific Storms. Here North Head forms a protective buttress in what is part of the Sydney Harbour National Park. Undaunted by the rugged terrain, rock fishermen risk life and limb on cliff tops or the more dangerous wave-washed rock platforms for the chance of a fresh fish dinner.*

78-79 *The south-east coast of Western Australia still carries a hint of the vast open plains of the Nullarbor with its rolling sand dunes, pink salt pans and empty shoreline as seen in Bremmer Bay dunes* (top), *Middle Island* (bottom) *and the mouth of the Donnelly River* (right).

80-81 *A pewter plate nailed to a post marked the spot on Dirk Hartog Island where a Dutch sea captain of the same name landed in 1616. Today the shallow inner bays are a haven for herds of dugong grazing on sea grasses on this isolated and beautiful eastern-most point of Australia. Free of land-based predators, turtles nest on the beaches.*

82-83 *Sculpted by wind and sea, some of the Twelve Apostles face the ceaseless pounding of the southern ocean on Victoria's rugged south coast. At night penguins shuffle up the beach to rest in sandy burrows after 14-16 hours at sea.*

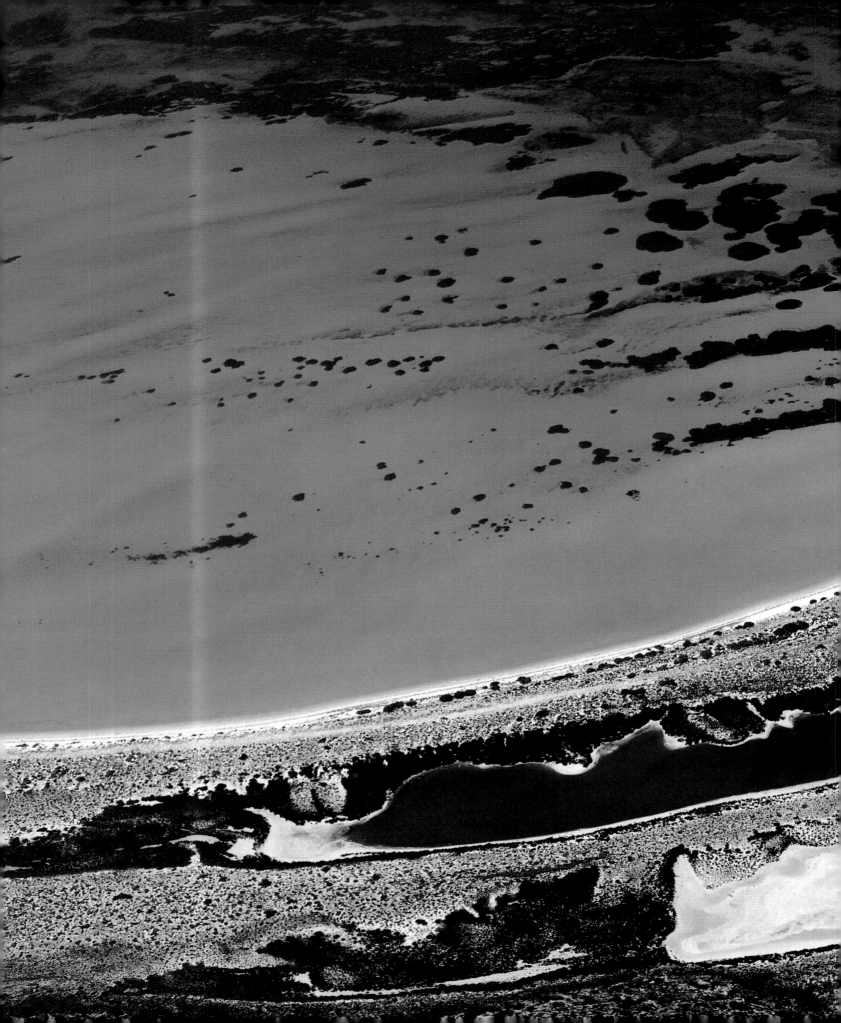

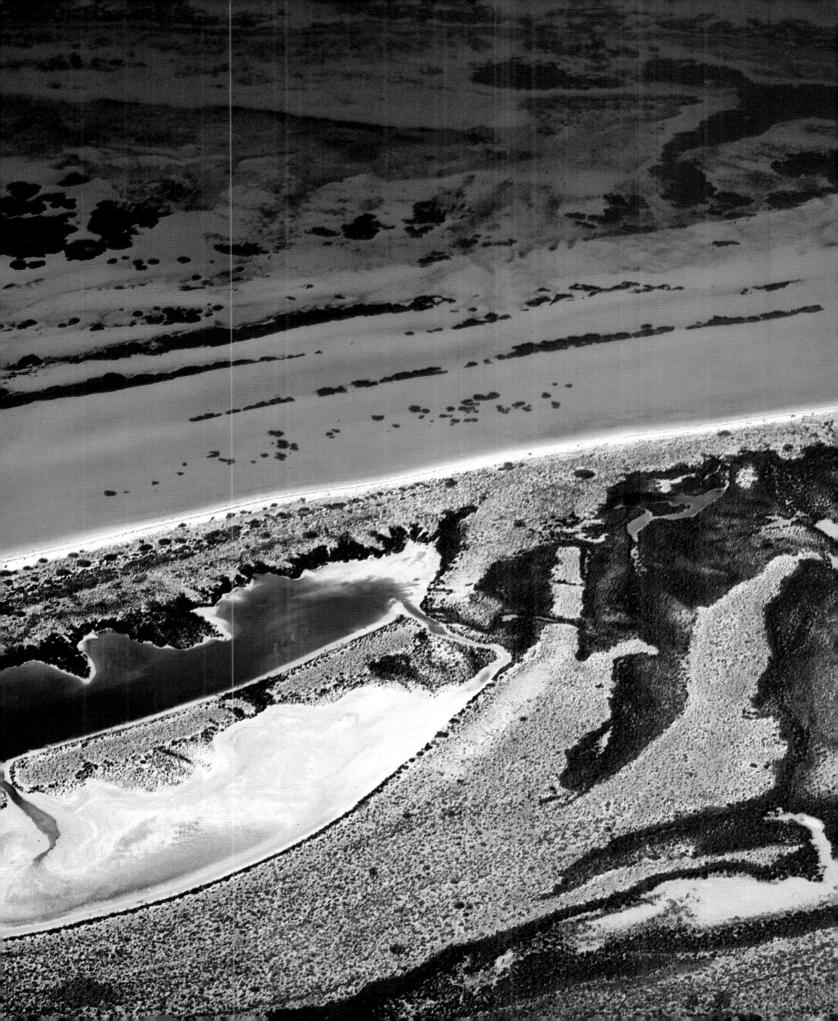

People and pastimes

84 *Leisure time and sport plays a big part in the Australian culture. Pensions, early retirement and a longer life-span allow plenty of time to socialise over a quiet game of bowls such as here in Darwin. A shortened working week allows the younger generation to gather every weekend to participate in locally organised sport such as this game of rugby football* (bottom) *in New South Whales.*

85 *After an early start, balloonists have almost finished preparations for a day of aerial racing. With clear boundless skies, unpolluted waters and open uninhabited plains, the Australian people have an understandable love for the outdoors. With modern jet travel it is easy to compare the Australian nation and environment with the older societies of the northern hemisphere with their overcrowding and pollution giving credence to the description of Australia as "the lucky country".*

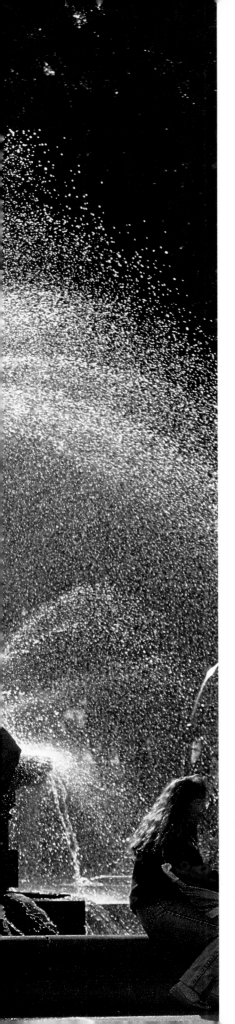

86-87   Hyde Park, in the centre of the inner Sydney commercial district, provides open space and towering native fig trees as cooling shelter in the summer sun. The Archibald Memorial Fountain is a popular resting and meeting place for office workers or shoppers looking for respite from the nearby city bustle.

87   On weekends Hyde Park offers space to contemplate in, such as at this giant chess game (top), or open grassed areas for picnics, joggers or ball games. On the north shore a short ferry ride to Manly Corso (middle) with its associated surf beach provides daytime entertainment while at night the local pubs celebrate their multicultural origins such as here at the Hero-Waterloo hotel (bottom).

88-89 *The Sydney Stock Exchange* (below) *jumps with activity when the quarterly Balance of Trade figures are released. With such rich resources as the minerals found in the copper, silver, lead and zinc mines in Mount Isa in Queensland* (top right) *and the world's largest rutile mine* (bottom right), *Australia has the foundation to become a force in the international trade markets. The wealth of the mineral deposits may be indicated by the largest company to operate in Australia: the mining giant Broken Hill Propriety (BHP) with operating turnover in the multi-billions.*

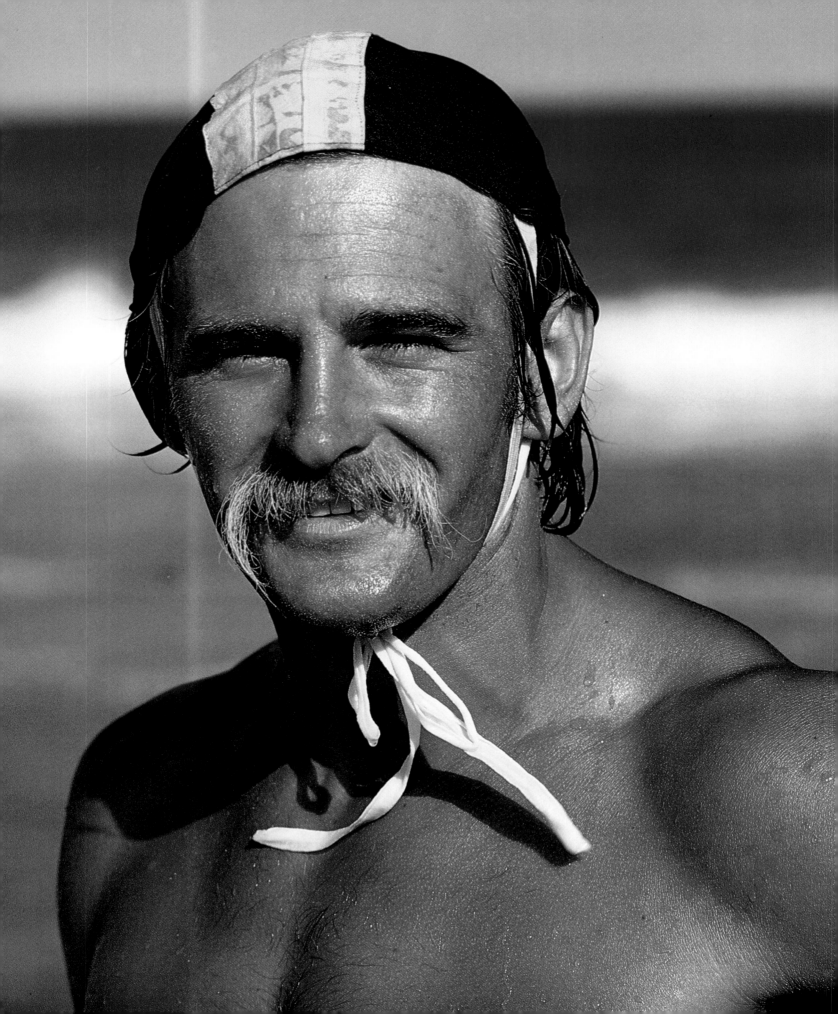

Sport, sun and surf

90 *The bronzed Aussie covered in salt spray while performing amazing feats of physical prowess on and in the water is an Australian trademark. Throughout the summer, surf lifesavers gather at local beaches to patrol popular swimming and surfing spots. Using their talents, competitions or surf carnivals are organised between local and inter-state clubs.*

91 *The surf boat* (top) *and paddle board* (bottom) *are two of the disciplines used in the carnivals to pick the fastest team. The most popular national competition is the individual "Ironman" contest.*

92 With countless stretches of ocean-front beach, it is no wonder that surfing (top) is such a popular year-round pastime in every state. Not content with local beaches and competitions, Australian men and women have competed successfully in international events. Windsurfers, such as these (bottom) battling the waves at Long Reef Beach in Sydney, also have similar international accomplishments.

93 For the more well-heeled, ocean racing in yachts has become an exciting sport, especially since the winning of the Americas Cup.

94-95 *Every year the start of the Sydney-Hobart yacht race on December 26th becomes a national spectacle. Crossing 621 miles, including the treacherous waters of eastern Bass Strait, yachts compete on size and class. Due to often tempestuous conditions, line honours usually go to one of the larger boats. While competition is keen in all classes, the ocean is the greatest adversary with many competitors paying the ultimate price in the changeable conditions.*

The Land: love and labour

96 top *Beef cattle thunder from a holding pen in central Queensland. While standard cattle breeds are successfully raised from Tasmania to Queensland, the harsh interior conditions have produced new breeds with the Indian Brahamans with huge horns and humped-back seeming to thrive in the conditions. Every few months the sleepy town of Keith, in the Wimmera district of South Australia, comes alive as farmers bring sheep from far and wide to be trucked to Adelaide and Melbourne.*

96 bottom *Newly shorn herds are graded and sold while the farmer nevously waits for the results.*

97 *Sheep farming in Australia goes back to the earliest settlers with the Merino becoming the most popular breed, here being mustered prior to shearing. With wool prices booming through two world wars, the industry now suffers from a glut in stockpiled wool competing with cheap man-made fibres.*

98 *Comfortable in his air-conditioned cabin, a farmer spreads fertiliser for the next maize crop on Mungadal Station. Despite modern farming methods this property in Hay, New South Wales, is as reliant as any on the whims of changing climate patterns affecting farms around the globe.*
While the eastern seaboard holds the bulk of the Australian population, the southern inland plains are dotted with huge farming tracts rivalled in size only by the wheat fields of the central United States of America.

99 top *Sheltered fertile valleys in New South Wales, Victoria and here, in the Barossa Valley in South Australia, provide perfect conditions for vineyards and wineries.*

99 bottom *Cotton harvesters gather in the ripened bolls on the fertile plains close to the western side of the Great Dividing Range inland from Brisbane.*

100-101 *Pausing for a late tea break, farmers talk about the subject closest to their heart: the land and the crop. When the crop and the weather are right, neighbours work together to bring in the harvest as quickly as possible. Shared goals, successes, and hardship draw country communities together in a comradeship common in farming communities the world over.*

Aborigines: caretakers of time

102 *Members of the Tjapukai tribe display traditional hunting boomerangs and spears. After centuries of discrimination, oppression and near genocide, Aboriginals along with many others are realizing the importance of retaining Australia's first cultural heritage.*

103 *Rock paintings dating back eons are a source of history and anthropological revelations that are missing from a race with no other written history. Depicting "Dreamtime" gods, common animals, hunting techniques, stories or parts of complex rituals, many important cave paintings that remain today are jealously guarded in National Parks with controlled access to prevent vandalism. From the Kimberley (top) and Kakadu (bottom) to the southern tribes of Victoria and Western Australia, rock paintings give valuable insight into the original Australian settlers.*

Cities of Contrast

104 top *With the construction of a new international airport, Cairns has expanded from a sleepy town into a city catering to tens of thousands of tourists visiting the Barrier Reef.*

104 bottom *While Cairns swelters in tropical heat, Hobart, in the southern-most state of Tasmania, nestles below Mount Wellington on a crisp winters day, demonstrating the contrasts found within the Australian continent.*

105 *Parliament House on Capital Hill in Canberra is the home of the Australian Federal Government. Comprising the Senate and House of Representatives, memebers of Parliament flock to the House when Parliament sits. Built with the express purpose of being the nation's capital, Canberra is stamped with the efficiency of design and the sterility of a blueprint missing in older cities with less noble beginnings.*

Sydney: birthplace of a nation

106 *Based on the shapes of segments found in a mandarin, the Sydney Opera House is a marvel of design. Plagued by controversy, disputes, budget blow-outs and political manoeuvring during its construction, the Opera House is now one of the "Big Three" to see in Australia, the other two being the Great Barrier Reef and Uluru (Ayers Rock).*

107 top *Buildings and architectural styles covering two centuries converge in Sydney. While split-second decisions are made in the commercial heart of the city, old-world time-keeping (left) remembers the beginnings of a thriving community. Bridge Street (right) blends modern glass towers with sandstone facades from yesteryear.*

107 middle   *The spires of Saint Andrew's Cathedral battle with utilities and insurance companies for space on the skyline.*

107 bottom   *On the eastern side of the city, Darling Harbour, with its modern structures and entertainment facilities, is accessed by modern mono-rail.*

108-109   *Sydney Harbour Bridge spans Port Jackson with the distinctive shape of the Opera House drawing attention to the modern success of Sydney. Contrasting with this is the fort or "Pinchgut" in the centre of the harbour. Its name comes from the convicts that were temporarily sent there on reduced rations as punishment.*

110-111   *Like shingles on a dragon's back, the tiled roofs in the suburb of Manly cover the peninsulas that shelter marinas and harbours on the north shore of Port Jackson.*

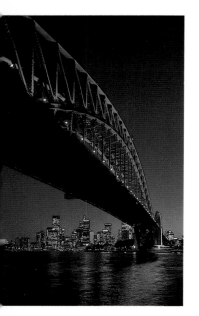

112-113 *By night Sydney flicks on a massive light show. Viewed from the north shore, Sydney Harbour Bridge* (left) *dominates the skyline. However the best vista is from the tower giving 360-degree views of the city and environs* (right). *Every night pubs, nightclubs, theatres and trendy bars cater to the desires of a young and eager city. Not just confined to the harbour, Sydney encompasses the industrial city of Newcastle 93 miles to the north to the steel foundries in Wollongong 50 miles to the south. While most capital cities accept direct flights from overseas, Sydney is the central point of most external departures.*

Marvellous Melbourne

114 *One unique feature that sets Melbourne apart from all other cities is the tram cars that provide transport in the city and most nearby suburbs.*

115 *Pride in her early architecture is evident in the many buildings retained to provide a fascinating contrast between old and new. Recently restored and refurnished, the Princess' Theatre has been the abode of productions from around the world since 1886.*

116-117 *Sitting on the northern shore of Port Phillip Bay, the city of Melbourne is the capital of Victoria, Australia's most populated state. Boosted by the early gold rush days and now by wheat, wool, beef, oil and gas, Melbourne continues to weather the storms of international trade wars. Once the capital of Australia before the construction of Canberra, Melbourne enjoys an on-going tussle with Sydney over the title of cultural and social leader.*

118 *Far from being parochial, the citizens of Melbourne crave contact with other countries and cultures. Possibly resulting from its richly cosmopolitan population, exhibitions at the Victorian Museum and Library (below) along with international art and cultural exhibitions are welcomed and enjoyed by her inhabitants.*

119 The English and European influences imported in Melbourne's early days remain evident in the architecture seen throughout the city. St. Patrick's Cathedral (top left) mirrors the era indicated by the Victorian Library facade as does the Malvern Town Hall (middle left) complete with avant-garde sculptures and the very British Melbourne Grammar School (bottom left). The private schools in Melbourne are imitations of the English system complete with uniforms and rowing teams.

119 right The War Memorial with its imposing facade becomes the centre of attention on 25th of April every year with the observance of Anzac Day. Returned servicemen and women from World War One to present day conflicts march from the city to the Shrine of Remembrance in honour of fallen comrades

Cities on
the coast

120 Workers paint the expanse of Story
Bridge crossing the Brisbane River. Built
on the riverbank, Brisbane is the capital
of Queensland with the Gold Coast to the
south and Moreton Bay at the river
mouth. Famous for its "Moreton Bay
Bugs" - a delicious, strangely-shaped
crustacean - and beaches, Brisbane lies
close to the New South Wales border and
heralds the beginning of the tropical
north.

121 Smaller than both Sydney and Melbourne, Brisbane city has only recently begun to benefit from foreign trade and capital. Primarily a business centre, the entertainment and gambling establisments that southern Queensland is noted for, are found outside of the city on the Gold Coast to the south.

The Gold Coast

122-123 *Mecca for sun-starved southerners during winter, the Gold Coast erupts with hotel and marina developments. Boosted by tax concessions for the retired and ripe opportunities for foreign investment, the southern beaches of Queensland have become a gold rush for property developers. Casinos, night clubs and bars beckon the sun-soaked tourists with the fall of dusk.*

124-125 *Perth welcomes the dusk with flickering lights of welcome. Standing next to the Swan River, Perth is the capital of the largest state in Australia and claims that the Fremantle Doctor, a stiff ocean breeze that springs up each afternoon, brings health and vigour to its inhabitants.*

126-127 *Surfers and paddle-boarders take advantage of waves swinging in from the southern end of the great Barrier Reef. Sitting well off-shore, the Reef protects the coastline north of the Gold Coast, pictured here, so that the area around Brisbane sports the only decent surf beaches found on the Queensland coast. Warm, clear, blue waters are a constant attraction to visitors from around the world, contributing to the image of wide open spaces and opportunity that typifies Australia.*

128 *Jabbing and clinching, a pair of male Kangaroos settle a dominance problem in a manner that gave rise to the description of "boxing Kangaroos".*